The Best Star

Published by Al

Copyright 2016 Alexey Evdokimov

Black and white version of the book

Content

The Best Star Wars Recipes 1
Introduction 2
1. Yoda's Green Sherbet Sundaes 3
2. BB-8 Donuts 4
3. TIE Fighter Ties 6
4. Super Bowl Ewok Guac 7
5. Grilled Cheese And Ham Solo Sandwich 8
6. Darth Vader Sausage Rolls 9
7. Yoda Soda 11
8. Jabba The Hutt Cake 12
9. Darth Double Dogs 14
10. Pit Droid Pizza 15
11. C-3PO Pasta 17
12. R2-D2 Berry Parfait 19
13. Star Wars Tie Fighter Snack 20
14. Ahsoka Pumpkin Muffins 21
15. Cad Bane Cupcakes 23
16. Chewbacca's Wookiee Cupcakes 24
17. Star Wars Cupcakes 25
18. AT-AT Cookies 27

19. Rebel Alliance Pumpkin Pie In A Jar 28
20. Star Wars – Blue Milk 30
21. Tatooine Sunset 31
22. Severed Wampa Arm Cake 32
23. Star Wars Chewbacca Smash Cakes 34
24. Revenge of the Sith Cake 35
25. Darth Vader Lightsaber Sugar Cookies 36

Introduction

Are you looking for droids, Wookies, humanoids, and other galactic beings to help create an amazing Star Wars party? Then you've come to the right place! Now Star Wars fans of any age can cook food that is truly out of this world. This intergalactic cookbook features healthy snacks, delicious dishes, sweet treats, and easy-to-use recipes that will entice even the pickiest eaters. Here's my rundown of some of most popular Star Wars recipes across the internet and the galaxy! All recipes with pictures. May the Force (and the food) be with you. Bon Appetit!

1. Yoda's Green Sherbet Sundaes

The force is strong with these adorable Yoda Sherbet Sundaes. Create your own Jedi masterpieces using green sherbet topped with green candy ears and marshmallow eyes.

INGREDIENTS

- Green sherbet
- Green taffy (we used "Summer Fruit Starburst"), 2 for each Yoda
- Mini marshmallows, 1 for each Yoda
- Food coloring pens, yellow and black
- Kitchen shears
- Ice cream scoop
- Cookie sheet
- Parchment paper

INSTRUCTIONS

1) Before starting, be sure that there is space in your freezer for a small cookie sheet.

2) Place parchment paper on top of a cookie sheet and then scoop balls of green sherbet onto parchment paper. Place the cookie sheet in the freezer.
3) While the sherbet is firming up, open two taffy candies and pull them to flatten. Use kitchen shears to cut a teardrop ear shape from each candy.
4) Cut a tiny round nose, a thin line for a mouth, and two crescents (for eyelids) from the scraps of remaining green taffy.
5) Cut a mini marshmallow in half and draw a yellow iris and black pupil on each marshmallow half using food coloring pens.
6) Remove the sherbet from the freezer and place each sherbet ball in a sundae cup.
7) Press the ears into the sides of the sherbet and decorate with the eyes, nose, and mouth. Serve immediately.

2. BB-8 Donuts

This particular BB-8 droid is edible, making it both useful and delicious.

INGREDIENTS

- Donut holes
- 12 ounces white candy melts
- Black icing
- Blue icing
- Orange Icing
- Lollipop sticks

INSTRUCTIONS

1) Melt candy melts according to directions.
2) Dip the donut holes to coat. For the top of BB-8, slice donut holes in half, then dip into candy melts. Place on parchment to set.
3) Once the coating has set, add details using a #2 tip and the blue and orange icing.
4) Use black icing and a #3 tip to add BB-8's eyepiece details.
5) When the icing has dried, poke the lollipop stick into the half dome and slide up the stick. Then poke the round donut hole below it to complete the droid.

3. TIE Fighter Ties

INGREDIENTS

- 4 pre-cooked sausages or hot dogs, approximately 5-inches long
- 1 package refrigerator breadsticks (8 breadsticks)

INSTRUCTIONS

1) Preheat the oven to 350°F.
2) Cut sausages in half crosswise. Set aside.
3) Open the package of breadsticks and separate the lengths of dough.
4) Cut the lengths in half and set aside. You should have 16 lengths of dough when you are finished.
5) Place one sausage half, cut-side down, on a baking sheet.
6) Take 1 length of dough and wrap it around the base of the sausage half. Cross the ends and let them fall on the baking sheet in the form of the letter V. Using another length of dough, wrap the same sausage in the opposite direction. Cross the ends and let them fall in the form of an upside-down V. Repeat with remaining dough and sausage halves.
7) Bake according to breadstick package directions, or until dough puffs up and turns golden brown.
8) Using pot holders, remove from the oven. Serve with ketchup and mustard.

4. Super Bowl Ewok Guac

INGREDIENTS

- 5 ripe avocados
- Bundle of green onions
- Bushel of cilantro
- 1 jalapeno
- 1 lemon
- Salt
- Clove of garlic (optional)
- Brown chips and crackers (My favorites are Casa Sanchez Totopos tortilla chips and Mary's Gone Crackers original crackers)

INSTRUCTIONS

1) The recipe is pretty simple. First, cut up your avocados, and throw them into a mixing bowl. Keep three pits and an avocado skin off to the side.
2) Finely chop the green onions and add them to the mix. Set aside a couple finely sliced pieces of onion for later use.
3) Chop up the cilantro and dice the jalapeno, too. I removed the seeds before chopping the pepper up to keep the guacamole from getting too spicy. But if you dig the heat, then throw the jalapeno seeds in there as well. You can also add a minced clove of garlic to give it an extra kick.

4) Squeeze the juice of one lemon into the mixing bowl, and set the rind aside.
5) Well, don't get all mushy on me. Actually — do! Even Han Solo would agree that guacamole is best as a big bowl of mush. So mash up the ingredients to your desired consistency, and transfer the guac into a serving bowl.
6) Remember those three avocado pits you set aside? Position the pits in the guacamole to give the Ewok two eyes and nose.
7) Take the avocado skin, cut out a cute 'lil smile, and position it accordingly under the nose. For some added character, place a few rings of green onion in the center of the eyes.
8) Stick your crackers into the guac to emulate the furry coat of our favorite woodland creature. To create the Ewok's ears, place two crackers onto the rim of your serving bowl using dollops of guacamole as an adhesive.
9) Finally, cut two little squares out of the saved lemon rind. Place them over the smile, and BOOM! Your Ewok's got teeth!

5. Grilled Cheese And Ham Solo Sandwich

INGREDIENTS

- Bread of your choice

- Ham slices
- Cheese of your choice
- Butter
- Millennium Falcon Cutout

INSTRUCTIONS

1) Spread butter on the outer sides of your bread slices.
2) Fill your sandwich with layers of cheese and ham.
3) Grill each side of the sandwich in a large skillet over medium-high heat. Once both sides are golden brown and your cheese is melted, remove from heat and let it cool a little.
4) Place Millennium Falcon cutout on top of the sandwich and cut your sandwich to match.
5) Now you have the yummiest hunk of junk in the galaxy.

6. Darth Vader Sausage Rolls

INGREDIENTS

- Shortcrust pastry - either homemade or ready-to-roll
- Pork sausage meat

- A little beaten egg
- Pastry cutters of your choice
- Optional: fresh sage or other herbs

INSTRUCTIONS

1) Firstly, preheat the oven to 400'F (200'C). Then you will need to prepare your filling. I like to add fresh sage to plain pork sausage. Finely chop the sage and then mix thoroughly into the sausage meat... as mucky as it sounds, the easiest way to do this is with your hands.
2) Next, you will need to either unroll your ready-to-roll pastry or use a rolling pin to roll it to approximately 1/8th inch or 3mm thickness. Using your cookie cutter, cut out an even number of shapes... if you are using the stamping type like me, you only need to create an imprint in half of them!
3) Grease a baking sheet, or use a silicone liner or baking parchment. Place half of the cut-outs (the non-imprinted half) onto the sheet making sure they are well spaced. Then using a pastry brush, carefully cover them in beaten egg, making sure to go all the way to the edges. You will then need to get a small dollop of your filling and shape it to fit the cut-out with a 1/4 inch (6mm) gap all the way around. Put it on top of the pastry cut-out on the sheet. Then egg-wash the underside of one of the imprinted cut-outs and place on top of the sausage meat. Gently pinch the edges of the two pastry shapes together, taking care not to change the shape too much or to squash the imprint. Once all prepared, use the remaining beaten egg to brush over the top layer. This will help them to go golden brown and to highlight the imprinted features.
4) Put the baking sheet into the oven and bake for approximately 20-25 minutes until the pastry is golden brown and the sausage meat is fully cooked through. These are delicious on their own or can be served with ketchup or mustard to dip them in! Yummy!

7. Yoda Soda

INGREDIENTS

- 3 limes
- 3 tablespoons sugar, or more to taste
- 1 cup sparkling water
- 1 scoop lime sherbet or sorbet

INSTRUCTIONS

1) Place 1 lime on the cutting board and cut it in half. Squeeze the juice from each half into a measuring cup. Repeat with the remaining limes until you have 1A cup juice.
2) Put the lime juice and 3 tablespoons sugar in a small pitcher.
3) Stir with a wooden spoon until the sugar dissolves. Add the sparkling water and stir until mixed. Taste and add more sugar, if desired.
4) Using an ice cream scoop, scoop up the sherbet and drop it into a tall glass. Pour in the lime water. Serve immediately.

8. Jabba The Hutt Cake

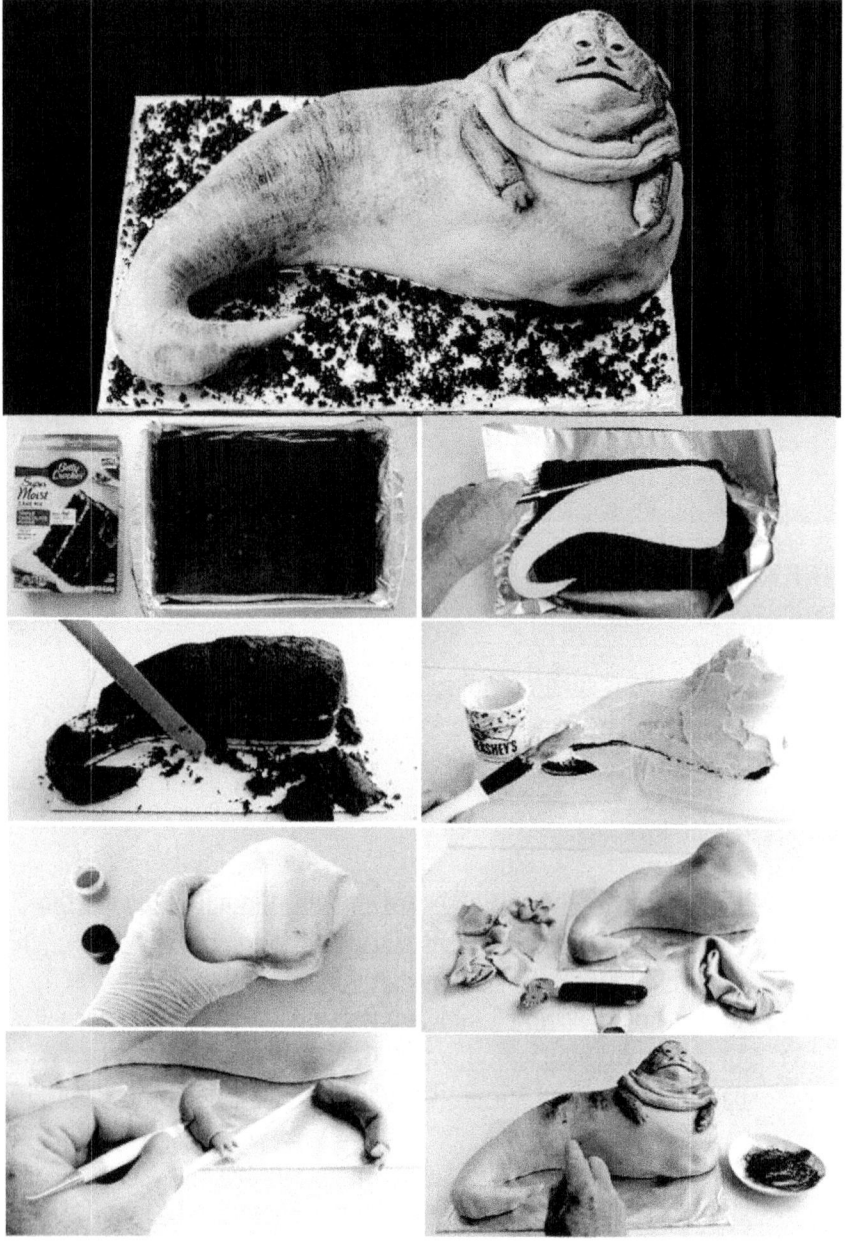

INGREDIENTS

- 2 Betty Crocker cake mix
- Eggs, oil, and water (needed for cake mix)

- 3 tubs Betty Crocker Hershey's Cookies 'n Creme frosting
- 40 ounces white fondant
- Green, brown, and yellow icing color
- 2 round orange candies
- 1 teaspoon Betty Crocker cookie icing
- Black food coloring marker

INSTRUCTIONS

1) Bake both cakes in 9x13 pans according to package instructions.
2) Cool cakes, then freeze for two hours.
3) Cut a slug shape out of a piece of coated cardboard.
4) Use slug shape as a template. Cut out a slug shape from each cake, cutting the end of the tail out of a scrap piece of cake.
5) Set one slug-shaped cake on the cardboard template.
6) Stack the second slug-shaped cake on top, with a layer of frosting in between.
7) Carve cake into a slug shape.
8) Add two more large pieces of cake, using frosting in between the layers, to create Jabba's upper body. Carve it into the correct shape.
9) Color and roll out fondant into a 24x18-inch rectangle.
10) Drape fondant over cake, smooth and remove excess.
11) Set cake on a serving platter.
12) Sculpt arms out of fondant and attach using a small amount of Betty Crocker Cookie Icing.
13) Sculpt Jabba's head out of fondant and attach to cake using two dowels.
14) Insert 2 round orange candies for the eyes and add facial features like a chin, nostrils, and mouth.
15) Roll remaining fondant out then drape over the head, allowing the fondant to fold into wrinkles around the head and arms.
16) Cut out eye slits, revealing the orange candies.
17) Add pupils to eyes using a black food coloring marker.
18) Add wrinkles and scratch marks all over body.
19) Paint with some green and brown food coloring to add dimension to skin.

9. Darth Double Dogs

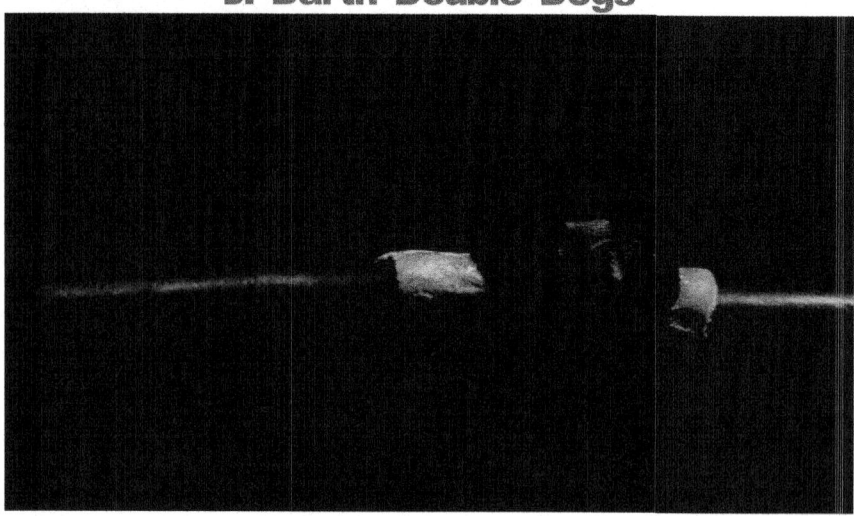

INGREDIENTS

- 8 foot-long hot dogs
- 1 package refrigerator crescent dinner rolls
- 4 long wooden skewers

INSTRUCTIONS

1) Preheat oven to 375°F.
2) Take a wooden skewer and skewer it halfway into one of the hot dogs, then take another hot dog and skewer it onto the other end. You will have one long hot dog held together with a skewer. Repeat with the remaining hot dogs.
3) Open the dinner roll package and unroll. The rolls will be perforated into triangular shapes. Detach them two at a time so you have four rectangles of dough.
4) Place one double hot dog on the edge of the rectangle, centering it. Roll the dough around the hot dog. When you get to the other side of the rectangle, gently press the hot dog down to seal the dough edge. Repeat with the three other double hot dogs.
5) Place hot dogs on a baking sheet and bake for 12 to 15 minutes, or until dough is golden brown. Remove from oven and allow to cool.
6) Serve with ketchup and mustard. Be careful when eating these — they are like a corn dog with a stick in the center.

10. Pit Droid Pizza

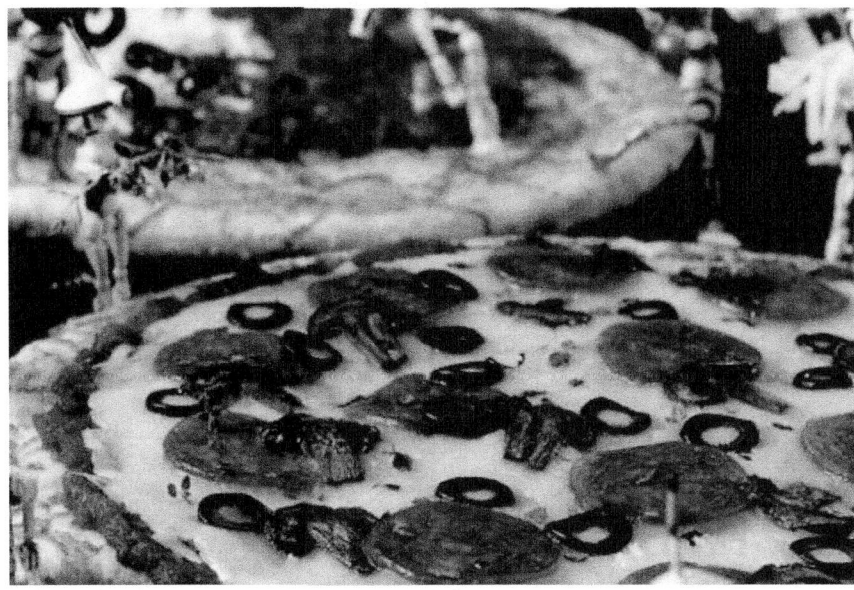

INGREDIENTS

PIZZA SAUCE

- 1 tablespoon olive oil
- 1/4 cup chopped onions
- 1/2 teaspoon minced garlic
- 4 tomatoes, diced
- 2 tablespoons tomato paste
- 1/4 cup water
- 1/2 teaspoon each dried basil, oregano, and thyme, or double the amount of fresh, chopped
- 1 teaspoon salt
- 1/2 teaspoon pepper

PIZZA

- 1 cup fresh pizza sauce
- 1 pre-baked pizza crust
- 1/2 cup mushrooms, sliced
- 1/4 cup black olives, sliced

- 20 pepperoni slices
- 1 cup shredded mozzarella

INSTRUCTIONS

1) Preheat oven to 375"F.
2) In a large saucepan, heat the olive oil over medium heat until hot. Add the onions and garlic and sautt for 6 minutes, or until the onions are soft. Add the tomatoes, tomato paste, and water, bring to a boil, then reduce heat to a simmer.
3) Cover the sauce and simmer for about 15 minutes, until thick.
4) Add the herbs, salt, and pepper, and stir. Remove from heat.
5) To assemble the pizza, spread 1 cup sauce on the center of the crust, leaving Vi-Inch or so around the edges.
6) Sprinkle half the mushrooms, olives, and pepperoni evenly on top of the sauce.
7) Sprinkle the mozzarella over the pizza.
8) Arrange the remaining toppings on top of the cheese. You may sprinkle additional herbs on top as well.
9) Bake on a pizza pan or cookie sheet for 15 to 20 minutes, or until cheese is melted and sauce is bubbly.

11. C-3PO Pasta

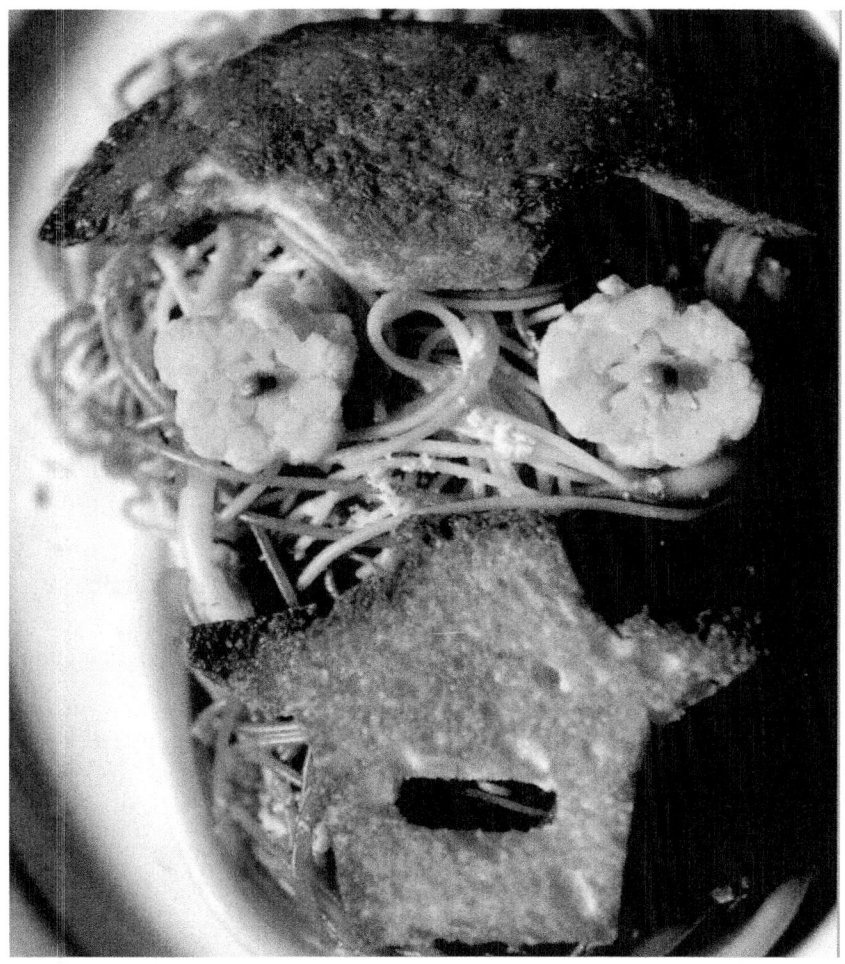

INGREDIENTS

- 4 ounces dried multi-colored pasta (cappelinl or spaghetti is best)
- 1 can (14 1/2 ounces) low-fat chicken stock
- 2 cauliflower florets (fresh or frozen)
- 1 cup water
- Pinch of turmeric
- 1 teaspoon salt
- 2 slices white or sourdough bread
- Olive oil
- Garlic salt

- 1 tablespoon parmesan
- 2 pine nuts

INSTRUCTIONS

1) Prepare the pasta according to package instructions.
2) While the pasta is cooking, pour the chicken stock into a sauté pan and bring to a simmer. Cook for 4 to 6 minutes, until the stock is reduced by half.
3) Place the cauliflower, water, and turmeric in a pan and boil for 5 minutes on the stove.
4) Turn on the oven broiler or toaster oven. With a knife or kitchen shears, trim one slice of bread into the shape of C-3PO's head plate and the other into a mouth plate. Brush both sides of each piece with olive oil, sprinkle with garlic salt, and toast in oven until browned.
5) When the pasta is cooked, drain and place it in a large bowl.
6) Pour the reduced chicken stock over the pasta and sprinkle parmesan and salt on top. Using tongs, toss the pasta until coated. Mound the pasta onto a plate in a face shape.
7) When the cauliflower is cooked, place the florets slightly above the center of the face for eyes. Place a pine nut in the center of each floret to make pupils.
8) Place the garlic toast head and mouth plates as shown.
9) Sprinkle with additional parmesan and enjoy!

12. R2-D2 Berry Parfait

INGREDIENTS

- Glass jar w/lid
- Small mixing bowl
- Spoon
- Vanilla yogurt
- Blueberries
- Raspberries or strawberries
- Blue, yellow, and red food coloring

INSTRUCTIONS

1) Start by putting 3-4 spoonfuls of vanilla yogurt into the bottom of the jar.
2) Next, put a layer of blueberries. Try to keep the layer of blueberries even from the front to the back so your layers stay straight.
3) Put another layer of vanilla yogurt (2-3 spoonfuls), then another layer of blueberries.
4) You'll need one more layer of vanilla yogurt (2-3 spoonfuls), then 1 more layer of blueberries.

5) Now, you'll need to make the vanilla yogurt grey for the top (and last layer) of yogurt. In a small mixing bowl, scoop 2-3 spoonfuls of vanilla yogurt. Add 5 drops of blue food coloring, 5 drops of yellow food coloring, and 5 drops of red food coloring. Mix the yogurt and coloring together until you get a nice grey color.
6) If the grey looks too dark, add 1 spoonful of vanilla yogurt at a time until you get a light grey color.
7) Then, put 2-3 spoonfuls of the grey vanilla yogurt as the top and final layer of your parfait.
8) Take a napkin, wrap it around 1 finger, and clean off a small space near the front of the jar.
9) Place a raspberry or strawberry in the clean space you just made. Your R2-D2 Berry Parfait is complete!

13. Star Wars Tie Fighter Snack

INGREDIENTS

- 2 squares graham crackers
- 1 large marshmallows
- 1/2 teaspoon peanut butter (2 small dabs)

INSTRUCTIONS

1) Use the peanut butter to "glue" the marshamallow in between the graham crackers. Kids can use a plastic knife to make their own. Fly your TIE fighter around for a bit; you can add your own sound effects. Enjoy!

14. Ahsoka Pumpkin Muffins

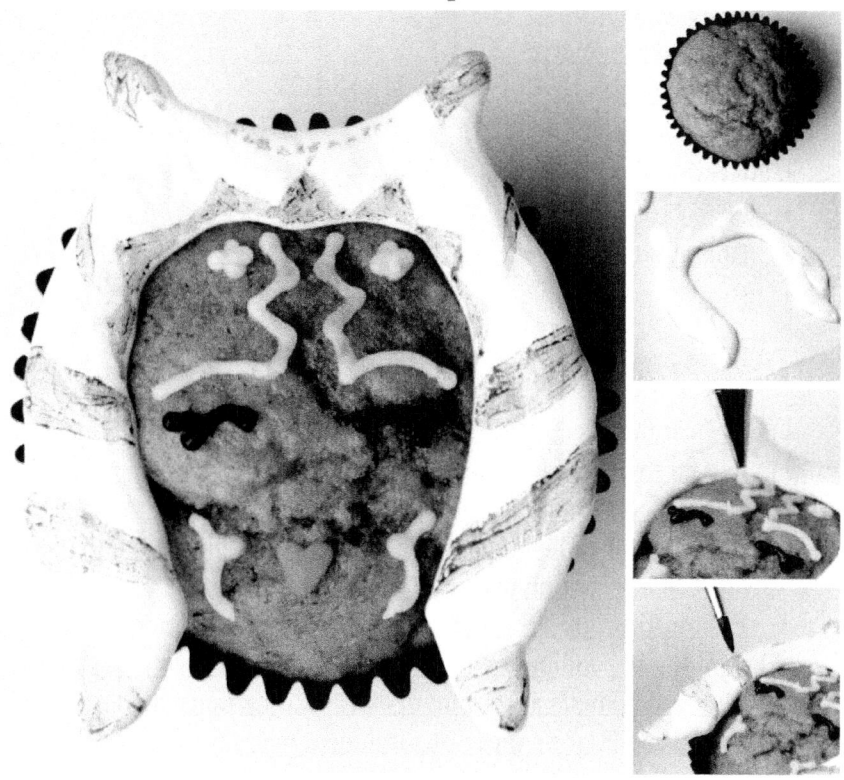

INGREDIENTS

AHSOKA PUMPKIN MUFFINS (MAKES 14 MUFFINS)

- 1 1/2 cups all-purpose flour
- 3/4 cup sugar
- ½ teaspoon baking powder
- ½ teaspoon baking soda
- ½ teaspoon ground cinnamon
- 1/4 teaspoon ground nutmeg
- 1/4 teaspoon salt
- 3/4 cup canned pumpkin
- 2 large eggs
- 1/4 vegetable oil
- 1/4 cup whole milk

YOU'LL NEED:

- White candy melts
- Black icing
- White icing
- Heart sprinkles
- Food brush
- Blue food gel dye
- Brown food gel dye

INSTRUCTIONS

1) Preheat the oven to 375 degrees. Prep muffin pans with liners.
2) In a large bowl whisk together the flour, sugar, baking powder, baking soda, cinnamon, nutmeg, and salt.
3) Make a well and add the pumpkin, eggs, oil, and milk into the dry ingredients, stirring until just combined.
4) Fill muffin cups 2/3 full with batter and bake for approximately 14 minutes, depending on your oven. Let cool on a wire rack.
5) Melt candy melts according to package directions, then pour into a piping bag. Place a piece of parchment over an Ahsoka template and pipe the white chocolate into the montrals shape. Place into the freezer to set, approximately 10-15 minutes.
6) Once set, take them out of the freezer and use icing to stick to the top of a cooled muffin.
7) With a #2 tip and black icing, add eyes and place the heart sprinkle for the mouth.
8) Using the white icing and a #2 tip, pipe on Ahsoka's facial markings.
9) With a clean food brush, use blue food gel dye to paint markings on the montrals and brown food gel dye to paint on the head jewelry.
10) Once the icing is dry, the muffins are ready to serve.

15. Cad Bane Cupcakes

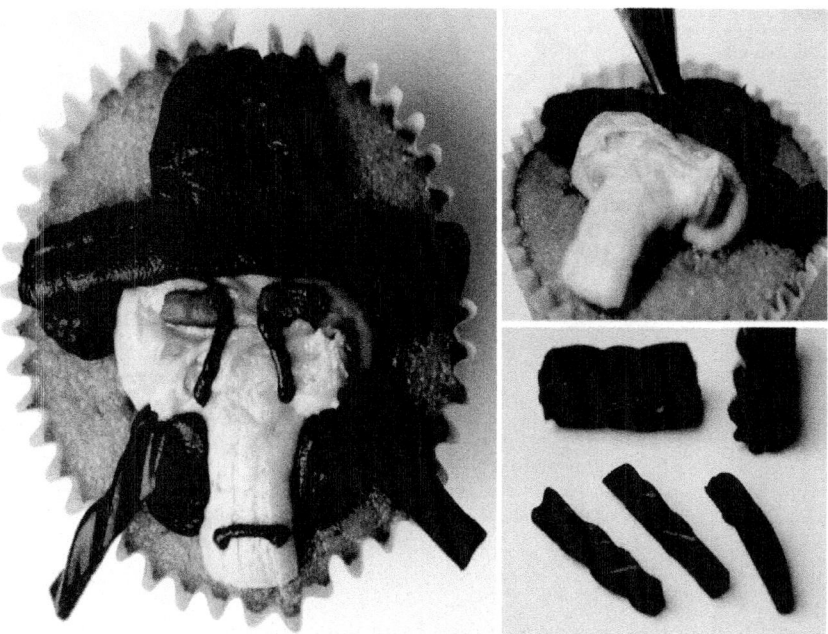

INGREDIENTS

- You'll need 12 cupcakes baked and cooled
- blue frosting
- black icing
- red icing
- black licorice

INSTRUCTIONS

1) Onto the cooled cupcake, pipe a T-shape using the blue frosting.
2) Use the black frosting to add his hat, breathing tube connections, mouth, and face lines.
3) Pipe red icing to add two eyes.
4) Finally, cut down two pieces of black licorice to replicate Cad Bane's breathing tubes.
5) Once the icing has set, the cupcakes are ready to serve.

16. Chewbacca's Wookiee Cupcakes

INGREDIENTS

- Chocolate cupcakes, baked from your favorite recipe
- Chocolate frosting, store bought
- White chocolate chips
- Brown soft chewy cand
- Black gel icing
- White gel icing
- Toothpicks

INSTRUCTIONS

1) Frost cooled cupcakes with chocolate frosting.
2) For eyes, press white chocolate chips, pointy-side down, into the frosted cupcakes.
3) Pull off two small pieces of brown chewy candy and roll them into balls. Press these onto the white chocolate chips.
4) Dab on black gel icing pupils, a nose, and a few lines of black gel icing in around his face.
5) Draw a small upside down U, using white gel icing for Chewbacca's fanged mouth.
6) To finish, pull a toothpick through the chocolate frosting to create the look of a shaggy coat of fur.

17. Star Wars Cupcakes

INGREDIENTS

- 1 box Betty Crocker SuperMoist yellow or devil's food cake mix
- Water, vegetable oil and eggs called for on cake mix box
- 1 container Betty Crocker Rich & Creamy vanilla frosting
- Ivory or yellow gel food color
- Decorating bags with tips
- 1 container Betty Crocker Rich & Creamy chocolate frosting
- Multicolored jumbo gumdrops (red, green, black)
- Miniature candy-coated chocolate candies
- Peppermint patty candies
- Pretzel sticks
- Candy eyeballs
- Black edible gel pen
- Black licorice

INSTRUCTIONS

1) Heat oven to 350°F. Bake and cool 24 cupcakes as directed on box.
2) In small bowl, tint 1 cup of the vanilla frosting with gel food color to make ivory frosting. Using photo as a guide, decorate cupcakes to make 5 of Princess Leia, 5 of Luke Skywalker, 5 of Yoda, 5 of Darth Vader and 4 of Chewbacca, or any other combination of characters as desired.

3) To make Princess Leia: Frost cupcake with ivory-tinted frosting. Fill decorating bag (fitted with regular tip) with chocolate frosting; pipe chocolate frosting on top of cupcake to make hair. For mouth, on lightly sugared surface, roll out red gumdrop to 4-inch circle with rolling pin, and cut out mouth; attach to cupcake. For eyes, add brown candy-coated chocolate candies. For hair buns, attach 2 peppermint patties, 1 on each side of cupcake, using small amount of chocolate frosting. Carefully pipe chocolate frosting on top of each patty. Repeat for as many cupcakes as desired.

4) To make Luke Skywalker: Frost cupcake with ivory-tinted frosting. For hair, on lightly sugared surface, roll out yellow gumdrop to 4-inch circle with rolling pin, and cut out for hair; attach to cupcake. For mouth, on lightly sugared surface, roll out red gumdrop to 4-inch circle, and cut out mouth; attach to cupcake. For eyes, add blue candy-coated chocolate candies. To make light saber, wrap top three-fourths of pretzel stick in rolled green or blue gumdrop, and stick in side of cupcake, or attach to side with small amount of frosting. Repeat for as many cupcakes as desired.

5) To make Yoda: Frost cupcake with untinted vanilla frosting. For face, on lightly sugared surface, roll out green gumdrop to 4-inch circle with rolling pin. Completely cover top of frosted cupcake with circle, and trim edges. Attach candy eyeballs with small amount of frosting. For ears, roll out another green gumdrop to approximately 1 1/2-inch circle, and cut in half; pinch ends of each piece to form ears; attach to cupcake, using pretzel stick. Using extra rolled-out gumdrop, cut small crescent-shaped pieces to add around the eyes, and add a small piece for the nose. Add additional strips along edges of face. Pipe on mouth using black gel pen. Repeat for as many cupcakes as desired.

6) To make Darth Vader: Frost cupcake with untinted vanilla or chocolate frosting. For face, on lightly sugared surface, roll out black gumdrop to 2 1/2-inch circle; trim to shape, and attach to top of cupcake. To make face, use black gel pen on top of rolled-out gumdrop. To make mouth, use black gel pen, or cut small section of black licorice; attach to cupcake. To make light saber, wrap top three-fourths of pretzel stick in rolled red gumdrop, and stick in side of cupcake, or attach to side with small amount of frosting. Repeat for as many cupcakes as desired.

7) To make Chewbacca: Switch tip on decorating bag of chocolate frosting to basket-weave tip; pipe sections of chocolate frosting on top of cupcake to look like fur. Continue until covered. Attach candy eyeballs, and use black gel pen for mouth. Repeat for as many cupcakes as desired.

18. AT-AT Cookies

INGREDIENTS

- 3 cups all-purpose flour
- 1/2 teaspoon baking powder
- pinch of salt
- 1 cup (2 sticks) unsalted butter, softened
- 1 cup sugar
- 1 egg
- 1 teaspoon vanilla
- Super Black food gel dye
- large pink heart sprinkles

INSTRUCTIONS

1) In a medium bowl whisk together the flour, baking powder and salt. Set aside.
2) In the bowl of an electric mixer cream the butter and sugar until combined.
3) Add the egg and vanilla and just one drop of black food gel dye. You want to make sure the dough is gray and not too dark.

4) Add the flour mixture, then turn the mixer on high until the dough pulls away from the sides of the bowl.
5) Separate the dough into two and wrap in plastic wrap. Chill in the fridge.
6) When you are ready to make cookies preheat the oven to 350 degrees and prep cookie sheets with silpats.
7) Roll out the dough to 3/8" thick and cut out the cookies. You may need to flour the cutter. Move to the prepped sheets and cut away the negative space of the dough between the legs.
8) Bake for 10 minutes and let cool on a wire rack.
9) Once cooled secure a large heart quin with frosting and serve!

19. Rebel Alliance Pumpkin Pie In A Jar

INGREDIENTS

- 8 (4 ounce) canning jars

- Rebel Alliance logo template
- 2 sleeves Oreos
- 8 ounces cream cheese
- 1 cup pumpkin puree
- 1/3 cup powdered sugar
- ½ teaspoon cinnamon
- ¼ teaspoon nutmeg
- 1/8 teaspoon cloves
- Pinch of salt
- 1 cup Cool Whip
- Cocoa powder for dusting

INSTRUCTIONS

1) Crush the Oreos until fine and spoon evenly into the canning jars.
2) In the bowl of an electric mixer combine the cream cheese, pumpkin puree and powdered sugar.
3) Stir in the cinnamon, nutmeg, cloves and salt.
4) Fold in the Cool Whip.
5) Spoon into the jars on top of the crushed cookies. Place in the fridge to set for 30 minutes to an hour.
6) Cut out the Rebel template and place onto the tops of the pumpkin mixture.
7) Dust with cocoa powder to serve.

20. Star Wars – Blue Milk

INGREDIENTS

- 1/2 cup milk
- 4 oz. 5% cream
- 6 oz. blueberry smoothie
- 1 heaping tablespoon white sugar
- 4-5 drops of neon blue food coloring

INSTRUCTIONS

1) Pour milk, cream, blueberry smoothie and white sugar into a 500 ml measuring cup. Stir well until all ingredients are incorporated and sugar disolved
2) Add 4-5 drops of neon blue food coloring. Mix well until evenly distributed.
3) Pour into class and enjoy.

21. Tatooine Sunset

INGREDIENTS

- 1 cup orange juice
- ¼ cup grenadine syrup (approximately)

INSTRUCTIONS

1) Fill a tall glass with ice and orange juice. Slowly pour in grenadine syrup and allow to settle on the bottom.

22. Severed Wampa Arm Cake

INGREDIENTS

- 6 egg yolks
- 3/4 cup white sugar
- 1-1/2 teaspoons vanilla extract
- 1 cup cake flour
- 1/2 teaspoon baking powder
- Pinch of salt
- 6 egg whites
- Red gel food coloring
- Powdered sugar for dusting
- 1 cup Guava jelly
- Whipped cream cheese frosting
- 2 cups sweetened coconut
- Chocolate bars

FOR THE WHIPPED CREAM CHEESE FROSTING:

- 8 ounces of cream cheese, softened
- 4 tablespoons heavy cream
- 1 cup powdered sugar
- Pinch of salt
- 1/2 teaspoon vanilla
- 1-1/2 cups heavy cream

INSTRUCTIONS

1) Preheat oven to 375 degrees. Prep a 10×15 inch jellyroll pan with parchment, lightly buttered.
2) In the bowl of an electric mixer, beat the egg yolks and sugar until light. Add the vanilla. Whisk together the flour, baking powder and salt and add it to the yolk mixture. While mixing, add in the red gel food coloring until combined. Set aside.
3) In a separate bowl whip the egg whites until stiff peaks form. Fold the egg whites into the red batter until combined. Pour the batter into the prepped jellyroll pan — using a spatula to even it all out. Bake for 8 to 10 minutes, depending on your oven.
4) Get a clean dish towel and dust it with powdered sugar. Turn the warm cake onto the towel. Peel back and pull off the parchment paper. Cut about 3 inches off the end of the cake and slice that into 1-inch-wide pieces — these will be the wampa fingers. Set aside for later.
5) Roll the cake up with the towel — the long way. What you are doing is trying to form the rolled shape. Let cool in the rolled up towel for 20 to 30 minutes.
6) Whisk the jelly to get it nice and loosened up, also reserve about 3 tablespoons for later. Guava jelly is light, almost clear and always makes for good "blood" substitute, but a dark jelly will work also. Carefully unroll the cake, and spread the jelly onto the cake. Now roll the cake up again. Quite obviously not with the towel. Place the rolled cake seam side down onto a platter. Arrange the wampa 'fingers' you cut at the end of a platter so they look like a hand.
7) To make the whipped cream frosting, mix together the cream cheese, heavy cream, powdered sugar, salt and vanilla in the bowl of an electric mixer. Mix until well blended. Set aside. In a separate bowl whip the heavy cream on high, just until almost stiff, not all the way. Add in the cream cheese mixture and whip up again. Don't overdo it, or you'll get a curdled look, not so pretty for cupcakes. Fold the frosting to make sure everything is incorporated.
8) Frost the cake arm and "fingers" with the whipped cream cheese frosting. Getting between the "fingers" can be tricky, so just use a small offset spatula and take your time. Take the coconut and pat it around the frosted cake and fingers, like "fur." For the fingernails I cut a thick chocolate bar into chunky pieces and placed them on the end of the fingers. Finally, take the reserved jelly and pour it on the cut end of the "arm." It will look like oozing wampa blood!

23. Star Wars Chewbacca Smash Cakes

INGREDIENTS

- CHOCOLATE CAKE
- chocolate frosting
- chocolate curls
- brown sprinkles
- chocolate brown icing
- tiny white heart sprinkles

INSTRUCTIONS

1) Bake the cake batter in small 4" round cake pans.
2) Once cooled, frost with chocolate frosting, and press the chocolate curls all around the sides of the cakes.
3) Add the brown sprinkles to cover the top of the cake.
4) Using a #12 tip, pipe a stripe of chocolate icing diagonally across the heart.
5) Add tiny white heart sprinkles along both edges of the chocolate stripe to complete.

24. Revenge of the Sith Cake

INGREDIENTS

- 2 cake mixes, prepared according to package directions shortening or non-stick spray or your favorite cake recipe
- small Pyrex mixing bowl or other oven-safe mixing bowl
- round cake pan
- 3 small loaf pans
- cake board
- aluminum foil
- 1 batch Buttercream Frosting, dyed red
- 1 batch Chocolate Buttercream Frosting
- candy rocks and pebbles
- red hots or other red candies
- red sprinkles
- chocolate bars
- Star Wars action figures (Anakin, Obi-Wan)

INSTRUCTIONS

1) Preheat the oven according to recipe directions.
2) Grease the small pyrex mixing bowl, the three mini loaf pans, and the round cake pan. Fill each 1/2 to 2/3 full with the prepared cake batter. Bake according to recipe directions. Since your cakes are

differing sizes, check often for doneness, starting at 20 minutes and then every 10 minutes or so after that. Cool in the pan for 10 minutes once you've removed them from the oven. Remove from pans and cool completely.
3) Wash and dry the toys well. Make sure no water is present in the nooks and crannies as this will mess up your frosting.
4) Cover your cake board with aluminum foil, if desired. Place your cakes on the board. In one corner you will place the round cake layer. Cover with a thin layer of chocolate frosting and top with the cake baked in the small pyrex bowl. This will be your volcano. Scatter your loaf cakes around the board.
5) Frost your cakes with chocolate frosting.
6) Pipe the red frosting from the top of the volcano down to the ground and then around the board for "lava" and spread it thinly with a knife or spatula. It doesn't need to be perfectly smooth; it's lava. Sprinkle red hots and red sprinkles over lava.
7) Scatter candy rocks and pebbles about. Kids love to do this!
8) Place chocolate bars floating in the lava.
9) Place your fighting action figures.

25. Darth Vader Lightsaber Sugar Cookies

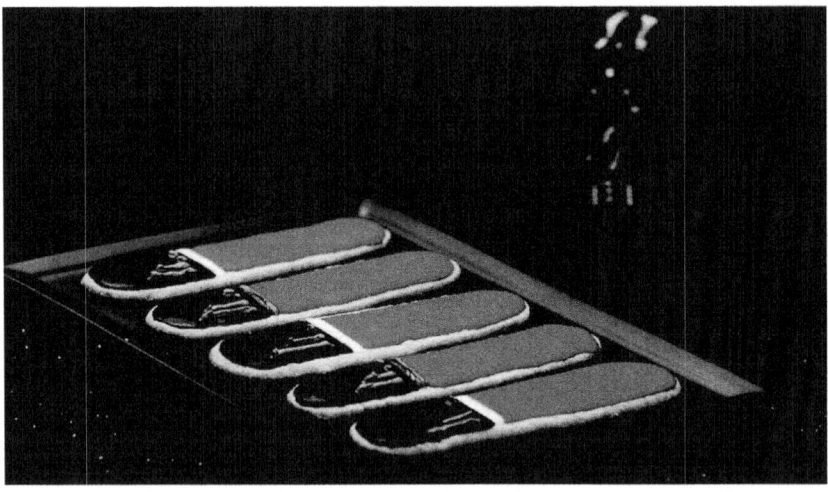

INGREDIENTS

- Pre-made sugar cookie dough

- Red, black, white cookie icing
- Knife
- Flour
- Bowl, medium
- Rolling pin
- Cookie sheet

INSTRUCTIONS

1) Put the sugar cookie dough in the freezer for at least 1-2 hours before you're ready to make the cookies. This will get the dough nice and cold and will make it easier to roll out later.
2) Prep a cutting board with some flour; this will help the dough from sticking. Take the dough out of the freezer and set a side in a bowl. Put flour on your hands to help the dough from sticking to your fingers.
3) Put the dough on the cutting board and start to roll it out with a rolling pin. Try and roll it out so the dough is about 1/4 of an inch thick.
4) Using a knife cut oval, lighsaber like shapes out of the dough. Just remember that pre-made cookie dough usually expands quite a bit so try and make them a bit on the thinner side.
5) Place the lightsaber cookies on a cookie sheet and bake according to the package directions.
6) When they're done baking, set them aside to cool.
7) In the meantime, heat the cookie icing according to the package directions.
8) Once the cookies are cooled and the icing is heated, start to draw on your lightsabers (as shown in the main image).
9) For the lightsaber buttons, you can use white cookie icing or you can add food coloring to the icing and make it grey before you draw the buttons on.

Printed in Great Britain
by Amazon